# BIRMINGHA...
# THE THIRTIES
# REVISITED

### Alton & Jo Douglas

Colmore Row, 1939.

ISBN 978-1-85858-543-7
Published by Brewin Books Ltd, Doric House, 56 Alcester Road, Studley, Warwickshire B80 7LG.
Printed by Bell & Bain Ltd.
Layout by Alton and Jo Douglas.

The Lord Mayor, Ald Horace Goodby, arrives to open the new Birmingham Municipal Bank, Alcester Road South, Kings Heath, 20th May 1933.

Front Cover: High Street, Erdington, 1930.

# C o n t e n t s

| Page 4 | 1930 | Page 46 | 1935 |
| Page 13 | 1931 | Page 55 | 1936 |
| Page 21 | 1932 | Page 64 | 1937 |
| Page 29 | 1933 | Page 76 | 1938 |
| Page 38 | 1934 | Page 86 | 1939 |

Page 96    ACKNOWLEDGEMENTS

# BREWIN BOOKS LTD

Doric House, 56 Alcester Road,
Studley, Warwickshire, B80 7LG
Tel: 01527 854228  Fax: 01527 852746
VAT Registration No. 705 0077 73

Dear Nostalgic,

"A Puzzlement" - sometime read the lyrics of this lesser-known song from Rodgers and Hammerstein's "The King and I". In it the King expresses his bewilderment at the changing world around him. But don't we all feel like that? Buildings have gone, behaviour, attitude and dress have changed and seemingly, without any warning, we have found ourselves much older. Well, we believe our books can help to restore part of that lost world and, at the same time, introduce younger people to the fascination of it all.

Another "puzzlement", for a lot of you, is where our material originates. As an explanation, when we completed "Birmingham in the Thirties", over a dozen years ago, we continued to search, mainly in private collections, for items from that decade as we do for every period. We were also given access to a large collection of postcards (one of the main forms of communication for many people in the thirties) and magazines as our network of contributors increased. Special mention must go to our friend Brian Matthews who has supplied us with, amongst other items, a cover picture for the last two titles. Sadly, over the years, several of our friends have passed on but we would like to think that we have done justice to their material. Anyway, the result, we hope you will agree, is a book of 400+ quite rare items - and life is less of "a puzzlement".

Yours, in friendship,

Alton

PS By coincidence "Birmingham: The Thirties Revisited" is also our 30th book about the city.

St Philip's churchyard, 1938. Known to many locals as Pigeon Park.

# 1930

Beaufort cinema, Coleshill Road, Ward End, c 1930.

The canopy of the Tivoli cinema is a much remembered feature,
Coventry Road/Lily Road, South Yardley, 1930.

Facing in the opposite direction, away from the city, the Tivoli can be seen on the
left, 1930.

Victoria Road, Aston, 1930.

Ernest Pinfold's, 1012 Coventry Road, Hay Mills, 1930.

The Green, Erdington, 1930.

Corporation Street, c 1930.

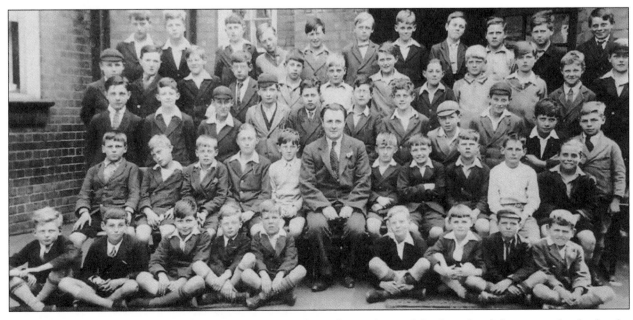

Acocks Green School, Westley Road, 1930. Two years later the Junior and Senior schools became mixed schools.

Colmore Row, c 1930.

Grand Theatre, Corporation Street, opposite Old Square, 1930.

Swan Hotel, Coventry Road/Church Road, South Yardley, c 1930.

Coventry Road/Muntz Street, Small Heath, 1930.

## SPLINTERS ARE DANGEROUS

An injury caused by a splinter in the hand or foot seems insignificant, but, if neglected, it can be a real danger. The splinter may have introduced dirt deep down in the wound.

The wound may turn septic and a whitlow—a painful affliction—may result.

When removing the splinter, use tweezers or forceps. Get a safe grip of the splinter and then carefully withdraw it. Care is needed otherwise you may break off the exposed end and leave the remainder in the wound.

After removal of the splinter, apply a hot fomentation to the wound.

## GOOD DISHES

## MADE FROM SCRAPS

Every good housewife is careful to see that nothing is wasted in her kitchen, and that no left-overs which can be made into different dishes, or used in some new form, are thrown away.

This applies even to the smallest of left-overs. One slice of ham, for instance, can be minced and used with scrambled eggs; the remains of haddock can be flaked and used in the same way.

In using up cold meat which is to be re-heated and served with fresh garnishings, or is to be minced or curried, remember that only a moderate heat is required and that the meat should be re-heated slowly, otherwise it will lose its flavour and be tough.

### Art of Selection

The art of making hors d'oevures, of course, is to place the right things together, so that they please the eye as well as the palate. You can learn quite a lot by experiment, and it is fun to try out new mixtures.

Cold cooked peas, and potatoes which should be sliced in oil and vinegar, go well with sardines and sliced hard-boiled eggs; or try sliced cold sausage with a salad made from left over cooked vegetables, which can be diced and mixed with mayonnaise or salad cream, in Russian salad fashion; some olives, prawns or anchovies.

Practically any vegetables can be put into a Russian salad—peas beans, carrots, turnips, asparagus or cauliflower is also good by itself with a little mayonnaise sauce poured over.

## HOW MANY BIBLES ARE THERE IN THE WORLD?

Seven in all. They are: The Christian Bible, the Eddas of the Scandinavians, the Five Kings of the Chinese, the Koran of the Mohamedans, the Tri Pitikes of the Buddhists, the Three Vedas of the Hindoos, and the endavesta of the Persians.

―――――――――

"Where did the car hit him," asked the Coroner.
"At the junction of the dorsal and cervical vertebrae," replied the medical witness.
The burly foreman rose from his seat. "I've lived in these part for fifty years," he protested ponderously, "and I never heard of the place."

## Mince and Curry

Even the smallest scraps of meat can be used up as mince; flavour the mince well and give it an attractive border of mashed potatoes, browned on top. For curry, the meat should be cut into dice.
For left-over vegetables there are many uses. They can be put into soups, but in summer-time perhaps we think first of salads and hors d'oeuvres.

## Salads

One or two left-over new potatoes can be sliced and added to a mixed salad; broad beans or peas are delicious in a green salad.
If you have a larger quantity of new potatoes or carrots left over, slice them and make them into a salad with slices of cold boiled onion pouring over a little mayonnaise sauce, or other dressing according to taste. And, talking of salads, don't forget that you can use up cheese, which has become slightly hard, by grating it over a vegetable or ordinary green salad.

## Hors d'oeuvres

Not only cold left-over vegetables, but scraps of fish or meat, and cold sausage in particular, can be used in the preparation of hors d'oeuvres.
But it's a good plan to have on hand such things as a tin of sardines, a bottle of olives or pickled walnuts, boiled anchovies or prawns in a glass jar.
You will also want hard-boiled eggs, or cream cheese, and of course you will like to use lettuce or tomatoes, beetroot, cucumber or radishes or anything else of a salad nature which will blend with the selection you have in mind.

The Blue Coat School, on the northeast corner of St Philip's Square, between Temple Row and Colmore Row, 1930. That year it moved to its current location in Somerset Road, Edgbaston.

Bull Ring, 1930.

Frederick and William Florence, Hay Hall Farm, Coventry Road, Small Heath, 1930. ASDA is now on this site. Incidentally, their smart attire confirms that they were on their way to a wedding.

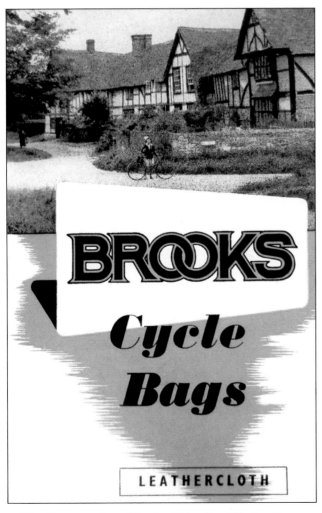

The firm was based in the Criterion Works, Great Charles Street.

Broad Street, 1930.

High Street, with a glimpse of the Roe Buck (left of centre) Erdington, 1930.

36/38 Bristol Street, c 1930.

Chatham Road/Bristol Road South, Northfield, 1930.

# 1931

St Martin's Church, Bull Ring, c 1931.

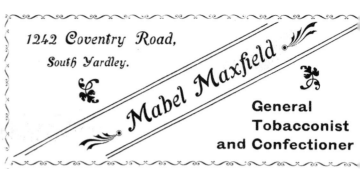

Paradise Street, 1931.

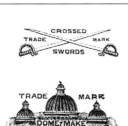

Refreshment Room, Platform 7, Snow Hill Station, c 1931.

The ford in Scribers Lane, Hall Green, 1931.

After the tornado, Coventry Road, Small Heath, 14th June 1931. It occurred at 3pm and was christened "Birmingham Bertha".

## 'QUAKE AND TORNADO HAVOC

### Birmingham Theory of Weakened Houses

## EXPERTS' VIEWS

Was the recent earthquake—the severest known in Britain—the real cause of the extensive havoc wrought by the whirlwind at Birmingham?

More devastation, Coventry Road/Charles Road.

– and Victoria Street/Green Lane, experiences the damage.

Charlie Hall, from Ward End, appearing in Laurel and Hardy's first feature film "Pardon Us", in 1931. Born in 1899 he appeared in almost 50 of their films.

Grange Road/Coventry Road, Small Heath, 1931. A projector and some of the seats from the cinema were later used in a miniature picture palace, in Shirley, rescued by the projectionist Albert Williams.

Bull Ring Cinema, Park Street. It started as the London Museum Music Hall and then Coutts Music Hall. It never converted to the "Talkies" and closed in 1931.

Portraits Painted
Artistic Photographs
& Enlargements

Herbert Holliday

The Park Studio
518, Coventry Rd.
Small Heath
Birmingham

COPIES OF THIS PHOTO CAN
ALWAYS BE HAD BY QUOTING THE NUMBER
BELOW OR IT CAN BE ENLARGED TO ANY SIZE &
BEAUTIFULLY FINISHED

No. 574

## THE USEFUL BREAST STROKE

The breast stroke is much too slow, grumbled a pupil of mine a few days ago. "It's all right to begin with, but nobody who can really swim uses it much do they?" I bridled visibly. "Nonsense," I retorted. "It's one of the most useful of all strokes, and sometimes I feel like scragging some swimmers when I see their appalling breast stroke style. Now you get into the water and swim three lengths."

"Breast stroke?" wailed the young man.

"Breast stroke!" I said firmly. He didn't do badly, but he made the same mistake that dozens of other beginners made. He concentrated too much on the outward kick and too little on the vigorous snapping together of the legs after he had straightened them. "Take full advantage of the drift between each set of strokes" I called out. "As you lie on the water with your body in one unbroken line, let it slip through the water naturally and easily."

I went on to explain that additional power could be obtained by the correct movement of the ankle joint so that the soles of the feet also played their part. "Let the soles push on the water!" I finished. "That's more than half the battle. Yes, yes, that's more like it. Easier, don't you think? Get your style right and you'll be getting that speed you're so anxious to have."

Harborne Charity Fete, 1931.

Birmingham's Jake Parker, captain of England's speedway team, 1931. He also set a new British Mile Record.

Opening of the Electricity Supply Dept. Shop, Holyhead Road, Handsworth, 1931.

Albert Ketelbey, born in 1875, in Alma Street, Aston Manor, wrote his Egyptian composition in 1931. His most famous titles were "In a Monastery Garden" and "In a Persian Market".

Belgrave Road, with Dares Brewery at the top, Balsall Heath, c 1932.

323/329 Birchfield Road, Perry Barr, 1932.

Wholesale Markets, c 1932.

The Chad Valley Co. Ltd. (manufacturers of indoor games and toys) Rose Road, Harborne, c 1932.

The Clef Dance Orchestra

o o o

All com's c/o Secretary Sidney G. Hull, 90, Westfield Rd, King's Heath, Birmingham.

Oscar Deutsch, born in 1893, in Balsall Heath, became President of Singers Hill Synagogue in 1932. He was responsible for the Odeon chain of cinemas and by the following year there were 26 in existence. His publicity claimed that "Odeon" stood for "Oscar Deutsch Entertains Our Nation"!

Multi-instrumentalist Teddy Brown, a regular at the Hippodrome, tests a modern light-weight motorcycle in Thorp Street, 1932.

The view from Yardley Parish Church, 1932.
Council houses would replace the farmland.

Bluebell Woods, The Lickey Hills, Rednal, c 1932.

Goods and grain warehouses, Camp Hill c 1932.

Eric Hollies, a Warwickshire stalwart from 1932. He was famous for getting Don Bradman out, in the Aussie's last test innings in 1948, for a duck.

Yardley Road, c 1932.

Clay Lane, Yardley, c 1932.

Aston Lane railway bridge, 1932.

The University of Birmingham, 1932.

The University of Birmingham, from Pritchatts Road, 1932.

BY APPOINTMENT

## KELLY'S DIRECTORY
OF

# BIRMINGHAM

(WITH ITS SUBURBS)

AND

# SMETHWICK

WITH A STREET PLAN ENGRAVED EXPRESSLY FOR THE BOOK

## 1933

### KELLY'S DIRECTORIES LTD.

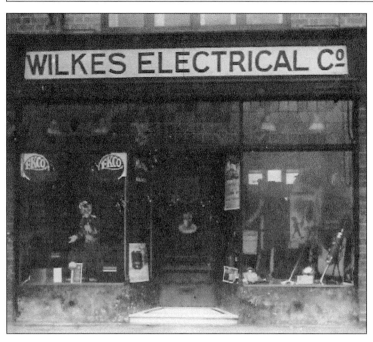

161 Station Road, Stechford, 1933.

Dunlop Rubber Co. Ltd. Fort Dunlop,
Erdington, c 1933.

Southall Brothers and Barclay Ltd. (manufacturers of surgical dressings) Charford Mills,
Alum Rock Road, Saltley, c 1933.

Acocks Green, 1933.

Old Square, with Lewis's extension under construction, Corporation Street, 9th March 1933.

New Street, looking towards Corporation Street, with King Edward's High School on the left, c 1933.

Trolley Omnibus, March 1933.

Stechford Road, Hodge Hill, 1933.

## •AN AFTERNOON WEDDING AT THE BOTANICAL GARDENS •

## CO-OPERATIVE EXHIBITION.

### OPENING CEREMONY AT BINGLEY HALL.

3.6.33

The National Co-operative Exhibition, which was opened at Bingley Hall this afternoon in the presence of many delegates and friends attending the Congress which starts on Monday morning next, is on ambitious lines and comprises exhibits which depict the many phases of the Co-operative movement and its manufactures, set in attractive and interesting fashion.

Starting from a bungalow designed erected and furnished by departments of the Co-operative Wholesale Society, there are more than 100 exhibits showing the growth of the movement, in addition to stalls of the many departments of Co-operative activity.

Apart from these, the attractions of the exhibition, which will continue until June 17, include continuous music by well-known bands, dancing demonstrations, and a Temple of Co-operative Industry, in which living models illustrate the productive side of the co-operative movement.

Mr. G. W. Brookes, a director of the Wholesale Society, who presided at the opening gathering, spoke with pride of the exhibition and mentioned that it was three times as large as that at Bournemouth last year and the exhibits occupied 16,000 square feet.

In opening the exhibition, Mr. W. Millerchip, of the Co-operative Union Central Board, said it showed something of the success of democracy in industry. He had been associated with the Co-operative movement half a century, and he invited them to look behind the intrinsic value of the goods they saw in that hall and they would realise the principles on which they had been produced and what those principles meant, if they were carried to their logical conclusion, for this country and for commerce and industry throughout the world.

A feature of the ceremony was the singing, by local children dressed in national costumes, of the Congress theme song written by Mr. Jack Jesson, a young Birmingham composer.

34    A new fountain, donated by employees to the company, Cadbury's, June 1933.

Domestic Science Class, St Paul's School for Girls, Vernon Road, Edgbaston, 1933.

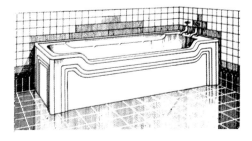

Birmingham MP (later Prime Minister) Neville Chamberlain visits 30 Hopstone Road, Weoley Castle, 1933.
It was the 40,000th house to be opened, in Birmingham, since the First World War.

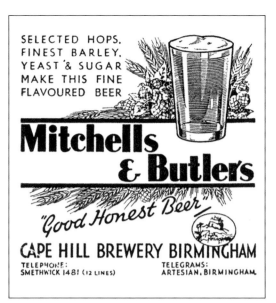

HRH Prince George (later to be King) and Lord Mayor, Horace Goodby, after the official opening of the Head Office of the Birmingham Municipal Bank, Broad Street, 27th November 1933.

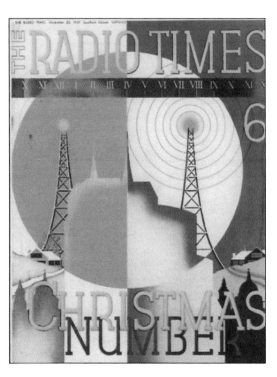

Dad : *Your mother says she'll leave me in the New Year if I don't quit buying Armstrong records.*
Lad : *That's tough, dad.*
Dad : *Yes, we shall miss her.*

# 1934

Coventry Road, looking down Church Road, South Yardley, 1934. This became known as the Swan Island.

Victoria Square, 1934.

Colmore Row, with Church Street on the immediate left, May 1934.

New Street, from the junction of Stephenson Place and Corporation Street, c 1934.

ARTHUR TIMS.     LES WOTTON.

TOMMY GAMBLE.    BILL PITCHER.    JACK CHAPMAN.    JACK ORMSTON (CAPTAIN)        WALLY LLOYD.

THE BIRMINGHAM SPEEDWAY TEAM. 1934.

Tom Dollery joins Warwickshire C.C.C. in 1934. He eventually, after war service, became the captain and played until 1954.

         Digbeth Midland Red Coach Station, c 1934.

Cambrian Wharf, the beginning of the canal in the city centre, (off King Edward's Road) c 1934.

Austin Works, Longbridge, 1934.

Cheese counter, Lewis's Food Hall, 1934.

The Prince of Wales (centre of balcony, wearing a hat) opens the Ashcroft Estate, Vauxhall, 1934.

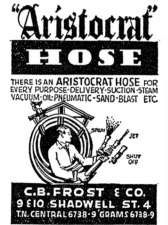

Cincinnati Machine Tool Factory, shortly after opening, Kingsbury Road, Erdington, 1934.

Red Hill, Coventry Road, Hay Mills c 1934.

RED ROBIN
4 OZS    4D
WINTER ASSORTED
TOFFEES
MANUFACTURED BY FILLERYS TOFFEES LTD. NATIONAL WORKS, GREET, BIRMINGHAM

Fillerys Toffees Ltd. was in Wilders Drive, Warwick Road, Greet and was incorporated on the 3rd August 1934.

Michael Balcon, born in Birmingham, in 1896, produces Alfred Hitchcock's, "The Man Who Knew Too Much", 1934. He was educated at George Dixon Grammar School and went on to be knighted in 1948.

Frank Cantell, born in Birmingham, in 1901, appointed the Deputy Conductor of the BBC Variety Orchestra in 1934. He had studied piano at the Birmingham and Midland School of Music.

Broad Street, with the canopy of The Prince of Wales Theatre showing c 1934.

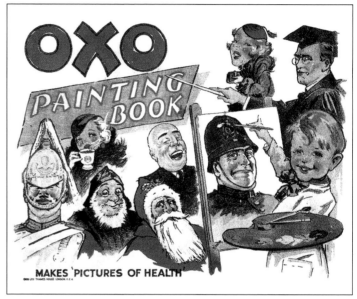

### AN AMUSING INTERLUDE

To while away an interval between rehearsals, Jack Jackson, the popular dance-band conductor, "accompanies" his H.M.V. Superhet Four-Forty, while Peggy Cochrane, another B.B.C. star, looks on. 3. 11. 34

A FITTING FOR EVERY FIGURE - - - A PRICE FOR EVERY PURSE

# COATS

## with luxurious fur collars for the colder days to come

Only at C & A can you possibly get such style, such value, such a selection of fashions, furs and fittings, at anything like these prices. This is no empty boast. It is FACT, based on commonsense. For C & A are FASHION SPECIALISTS—fashion our one and only concern. Moreover, C & A are the largest fashion specialists in the country, a fact that must logically be reflected in our prices.

**C & A MODES LIMITED** Regd.

The fur is dyed squirrel lock, very soft and lovely and used here with smart effect. You will see that furred sleeves are right back in favour. **79/11**

### SPECIAL ATTENTION GIVEN to the SMALL FIGURE

One of our famous small size coats, mounted with a strikingly lovely collar of pointed long lamb. Back is smartly panelled. **69/11**

The high-neck fastening, slim slotted scarf of dyed squirrel, vertical pin-tucks . . . all are definitely heightening. **59/11**

Fur revers are very popular this year. These are dyed marmot. Panels of pin-tucking at back give desired effect of height. **49/11**

A glorious collar of real Canadian fox, exceptionally soft and flattering, and mounted in ultra-modern style. Highest class material and workmanship throughout. **5 GNS**

**PERSONAL SHOPPERS ONLY**

**OPEN SATURDAYS until 8 p.m.**

### C & A OUTSIZES ARE SCIENTIFICALLY DESIGNED

A coat that owes its inspiration to the army. Cut with true military briskness, belted, buttoned and jauntily collared. The collar is trimmed with real Indian lamb. **89/11**

Imagine the luxury of this magnificent squirrel collar—so soft and rich-toned! It forms a perfect finish to the slim line of the coat. Lined with art. morocain. **6½ GNS**

Dignity is the first essential of an outsize. Next, a slimming line. This combines the two. Collar is trimmed squirrel lock. **59/11**

Here's a magnificent collar of dyed fox, perfectly suited to the quiet dignity of the coat. Sleeve detail is very smart. **5½ GNS**

Another of our famous slimming designs. Interest lies in the collar, one of the new broad cross-overs in flank musquash. **4 GNS**

# C & A MODES LTD · CORPORATION ST · BIRMINGHAM

Also at London (6 branches), Manchester, Liverpool, Leeds, Sheffield, Glasgow, Newcastle

1250 Coventry Road, Hay Mills, 1935.

Joseph Lucas Ltd., Great Hampton Street, 1935. Work on the extension is taking place.

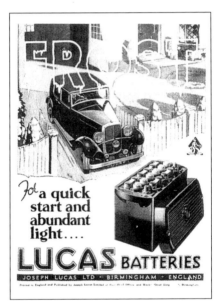

Employees of Joseph Lucas Ltd. leave work, Little King Street, (later Great King Street) Hockley, 1935.

The Joseph Lucas Works Band, 1935.

Silver Jubilee Party, Reginald Road, Saltley, May 1935. Commemorating the anniversary of the wedding of King George V and Queen Mary.

Corporation Street, from Stephenson Place, 1935.

Imperial Arcade, Dale End, 1935. The following year the clock was moved to the Market Hall, in the Bull Ring. It was destroyed, by enemy action, on 25th August 1940.

City Arcade, off Union Street, 1935.

1st Kings Norton Guides, Cotteridge School, c 1935.

Kings Norton-born actor, Brian Aherne, with Joan Crawford, 1935.

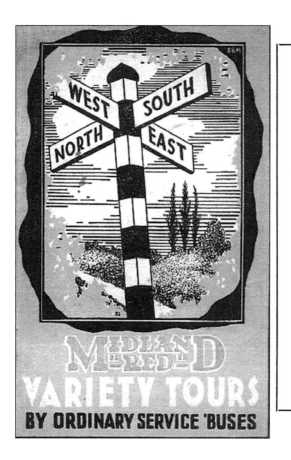

Albert Street/High Street, c 1935.

Hanging Lane, from Tessall Lane, 1935. Tessall Farm is on the left.

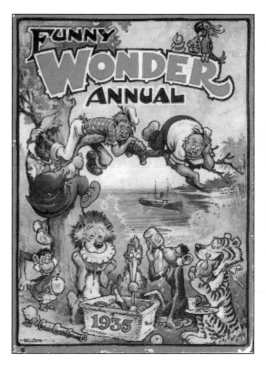

Central Fire Station, Corporation Street/Aston Street, opened by the Duke of Kent, 2nd December 1935.

The Town Hall, 1936.

Edgbaston Reservoir, c 1936.

Rose and Crown, The Lickeys, 1936.

Victoria Square, 1936.

Fox Hollies Road, Hall Green, 1936.

Handsworth Park, 1936.

Bournville Village Green, 1936.

Kewstoke Convalescent Home for Women, Kewstoke, Weston-Super-Mare, 1936. This was a haven for recuperating city people via The Birmingham Hospital Saturday Fund.

Kewstoke's Dining Room.

Bill Brindley, a popular entertainer from Nechells,
c 1936.

HIPPODROME
BIRMINGHAM
7 TWICE NIGHTLY 9
MATINEE EVERY THURSDAY AT 2,30

WANT SOMETHING FRESH?
HEAR AMBROSE IN
LIFEBUOY TOILET SOAP'S
RADIO SHOW

Bright as Spring flowers, or the holiday spirit: gayer than the lark, welcome as an entirely new Strauss waltz — that's what Lifebuoy Toilet Soap's new programme is like!
Ambrose and his orchestra play for you. Miss Evelyn Dall sings for you, inimitably. For half - an - hour music and light-heartedness fill the air.
So don't forget. Tune in to Radio Luxembourg at 6.0 this Sunday. Then tune in at the same hour every Sunday of the year.
And, if you want to ensure complete *personal* freshness, don't ever forget your Lifebuoy Toilet Soap!

Every Sunday at 6 P.M.
from RADIO LUXEMBOURG
WAVE LENGTH 1304 METRES

Imperial Hotel, Temple Street, c 1936.

Castle Square, Weoley Castle, 1936.

Broadyates Road, Yardley, c 1936.

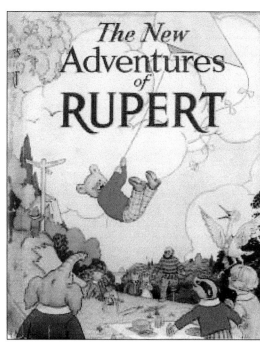

Park Lane/Potters Hill, Aston, c 1936.

New Street, December 1936.

Bristol Road, Selly Oak, 1937.

England's Second City is the world's most comprehensive manufacturing centre, and the obvious location for any industry related to its 1,200 trades.

Birmingham possesses unequalled transport facilities, abundant skilled labour, factories to rent, and sites for sale.

And for the tourist Birmingham is the key position for visiting the beautiful Midlands of England.

ISSUED BY THE CITY OF BIRMINGHAM INFORMATION BUREAU

Write for free literature to
CITY OF BIRMINGHAM INFORMATION BUREAU,
COUNCIL HOUSE, BIRMINGHAM, 1

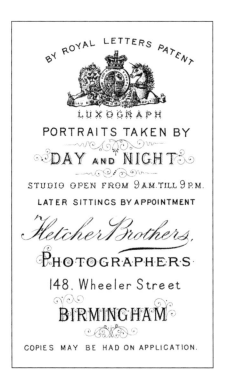

Woolworth's staff, led by Manager, Clifford Quatermaine, Stratford Road, Sparkhill, 1937.

194/6 Alum Rock Road, next to Thomas Baines (baker), Saltley, 1937.

# CORONATION OF GEORGE VI AND ELIZABETH
## 12th May, 1937

CORPORATION STREET

NEW ST

COLMORE ROW

HIGH ST

COLMORE ROW

BULL ST

# THE CORONATION
## A TRIBUTE OF PAGEANTRY
## BIRMINGHAM 1937

Decorated for the Coronation, Lucas's, Great King Street, Hockley, 12th May 1937.

New Street, dressed up for the Coronation, May 1937.

A coach all ready for the Coronation trip to London, May 1937.

A few of the National Flags on display.

The Market Hall, decorated for the Coronation, Bull Ring, May 1937.

The Green, Kings Norton, 1937.

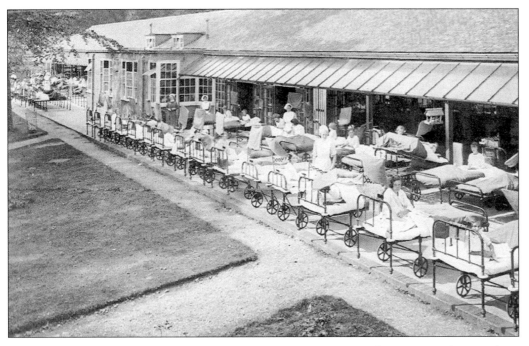

Royal Cripples Hospital, Bristol Road South, Northfield, 1937. It is now the Royal Orthopaedic Hospital.

Leon Salberg ran the Alexandra Theatre from 1911 until his retirement in 1937.

Derek Salberg, Leon's son, took over in 1937. He remained in charge for the next 40 years.

R E S Wyatt, captain of the Warwickshire County side from 1930 to 1937. He was also England's captain on 16 occasions.

Henry Hall and his Orchestra appear at the Hippodrome, 1937.

THE B.B.C. has decided that there is too much "crooning" in the dance music programmes. From next Monday the proportion of vocal items is to be cut down to one in three of the numbers broadcast.

This instruction has been given to the leaders of all dance bands.

At present crooning varies in individual bands and often several numbers in succession have vocal refrains.

The Jack Hylton Orchestra on TV, 1937. The problem is that very few people had television sets before the war.

Wagon & Horses, Wagon Lane/Coventry Road, Barrows Lane, Sheldon, 1937.

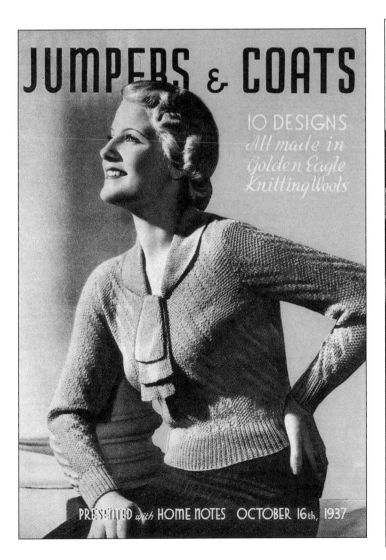

JUMPERS & COATS

10 DESIGNS
*All made in Golden Eagle Knitting Wools*

PRESENTED *with* HOME NOTES OCTOBER 16th, 1937

JRR Tolkien, after living most of his early life in Kings Heath and Hall Green, writes "The Hobbit" in 1937. Born in 1892, he was educated at King Edward's School.

### ENQUIRIES

**Brown, Mrs.** Wakefield.—Formerly of Burlington Road, Nottingham, believed to have left there six or seven years ago to live at a hydro in one of the suburbs of Birmingham. Old friend, Miss Croger, enquires.

**Cooper, George.** — Left Middlemore Homes about 50 years ago; last heard of about 35 years ago at Toronto, Ontario. Sister Harriet enquires.

**Cope, Charles.**—Lived in Erasmus Road, Sparkbrook, in 1885. Harry Brittain enquires.

**Edwards, Mr. W. S.**—Represented in 1924 a Cardiff firm of wholesale printers; believed to have come to live in Birmingham. Brother Jack anxious to hear from him.

**Gay, Mrs. George** (nee Minnie Morris).—Lived in Witton Road, Aston, about 1900. Old friend Florrie, formerly of Dolman Road, Aston, would like to hear from her.

**Goodhead, Mrs.** (nee Andrews).—Recently arrived in England from Tasmania. Ailie, of the old S.O. Bournville, would like news of her.

**Holland, Mrs. Emmie** (nee Judge).—Last heard of in Birmingham about 13 years ago; husband a butcher. Cousin Mabel in U.S.A. enquires.

## Our Forthcoming Serial.

# Handmaid to Fame

The Editor of the "Birmingham Weekly Post" announces with pleasure that he has secured the rights of the latest novel by the famous author

## BERTA RUCK

for serial publication. Previous stories by Miss Ruck have proved among the most popular that have appeared in these columns and this most recent of the products of her fertile pen compares favourably in romance, interest and entertainment with "Love on Second Thoughts," and "Sunburst," both of which have been recently serialised in the "Birmingham Weekly Post."

The heroine of "HANDMAID TO FAME" is, when the story opens, a private secretary to a middle-aged Member of Parliament. At 27 she is a humdrum sort of person. A "shy, colourless, uninteresting dear," is how her only male friend describes her.

And then things begin to happen. Her M.P. dies, her widowed father embarks on a second marriage and the family home is broken up. She becomes private secretary to an "idol of the films," and the whole course of her life is changed. Succeeding events are narrated with great verve and gusto, and, in addition to providing an abundance of romance and excitement, the story affords many an intimate glimpse of life behind the scenes as it is lived by screen "stars."

*The first instalment of "Handmaid to Fame" will appear in the*

# "Birmingham Weekly Post"

## on FRIDAY NEXT, DECEMBER 31.

Bull Street, 1938.

Bridge Street, 1938.

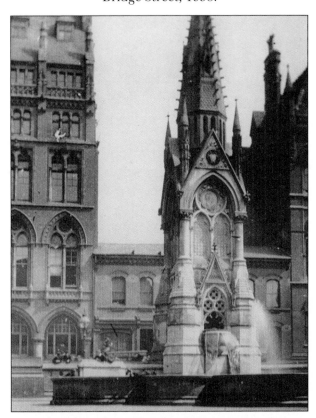

Chamberlain Memorial Fountain, Chamberlain Square, with Mason College in the background, c 1938.

## BOURNVILLE BROTHERHOOD

Mr. J. G. Milnes, always a welcome speaker at the Brotherhood, gave the address last Sunday, which was full of great interest. His subject being that of the misunderstanding of our fellows, and the principle of Divine Judgment, with its admonitions on the one side and its great consideration on the other.
Musical items were given by the orchestra, conducted by Mr. A. G. Barker. Mr. Howard a vice-president, presided in the absence of Mr. Daniel Roy, who was indisposed.

Dealing with customers' accounts, Cadbury's General Office, Bournville, 1938.

Packing chocolate assortments, Cadbury's, 1938.

Front Row (left to right) : Nurses F. E. Broadhurst and E. C. Bruce (in charge of Cadets), Miss D. A. Cadbury, Mrs. T. Oliver Lee (Lady Corps Supt.), Miss F. M. Dunscombe (Lady Divisional Supt.), Miss E. M. Howe (formerly Lady Ambulance Officer), Nurse G. Haime (Hon. Treas.), Nurse M. A. Hares (Hon. Sec.)

Cadbury's Nursing Division, nurses and cadets, 1938.

The University of Birmingham, Edgbaston, 1938.

The original Fircroft College, Oak Tree Lane, Selly Oak, 1938. It closed, due to the war, the following year.

THE LORD MAYOR
COUNCILLOR ERNEST ROBERT CANNING, J.P.
*Photo: Percy Wynne*

THE LADY MAYORESS
MRS. E. R. CANNING, GRAND MISTRESS OF THE ROBES
*Photo: Whitlock*

Preparing for the Pageant of Birmingham, Cambridge Street, July 1938.

Re-enacting the Restoration, Pageant of Birmingham, Aston Park, 11th July 1938. A part of the city's centenary celebrations.

## The Pageant of Birmingham

Episodes I—VII  *Scenario by* S. C. Kaines Smith

Episode VIII *including Grand Finale devised and arranged by* H. Gordon Toy

### CENTENARY CELEBRATIONS

#### PAGEANT COMMITTEE

*Chairman :* Councillor Rigby

THE LORD MAYOR—Councillor E. R. Canning, J.P.

THE LADY MAYORESS  Mrs. E. R. Canning

Alderman Roberts, J.P.
,,  Ager
,,  Miss Bartleet, O.B.E., J.P.
,,  Sir John Burman, J.P.
,,  Crump, J.P.
,,  Gelling, J.P.
,,  Kenrick
,,  Morland
Councillor Giles
,,  Richardson
Professor Bodkin
Mr. H. M. Cashmore
The Chief Constable
Col. Sir Bertram Ford
Mr. Sam Harrison
Dr. P. D. Innes
Sir Barry Jackson

Mr. Kaines Smith
Mr. E. S. White
Mr. Frank Jones
Mr. T. C. Kemp
Mr. H. Gordon Toy
Mr. C. Elliott
Professor Hely-Hutchinson
Dr. MacMahon
Mr. G. D. Cunningham
Mr. Eric Bloss
Mr. Sidney Taunton
Mrs. G. P. Achurch
Miss Barling
Miss Gwen Lally
Mr. H. H. Holden
Mr. W. L. Barber

#### PAGEANT OFFICIALS

*Pageant Master*—Gwen Lally

*Scenario Author (Episodes I-VII)*  S. C. Kaines Smith, M.A.

| | | | |
|---|---|---|---|
| *Business Manager* : | C. Elliott, F.S.I. | *Assistant Property Masters* | Gordon Phillips |
| *Chief Stage Manager* : | H. Gordon Toy | | Fred Bartlett |
| *Mistress of the Robes* : | Jean Campbell | | Joan Pegler |
| *Wardrobe Mistress* : | Ann Fisher | *Grand Master of the Horse* Brennan De Vine | |
| *Chief Designer* : : | Pegaret Keeling | *Grand Master of the Music* G. D. Cunningham | |
| *Assistant Designers* : | Estelle Morris | *Conductor of the Orchestra* Harold C. Gray | |
| | Betty Slade | *Master of the Arena* : | J. R. Keyte |
| | Althea Charles | *Mistress of the Dance* | Kathleen Danetree |
| | Gwen Carlier | *Publicity Manager* : | L. W. Faulkner |
| *Chief Property Master* : | Bernard Coaling | *Press Manager* : : | F. W. Bradnock |
| | | *Recruiting Manager* : | Baden F. Bradbury |
| *General Assistant* : | John Richardson | | |

A fearsome contributor to the Pageant, Cambridge Street/Crescent Wharf.

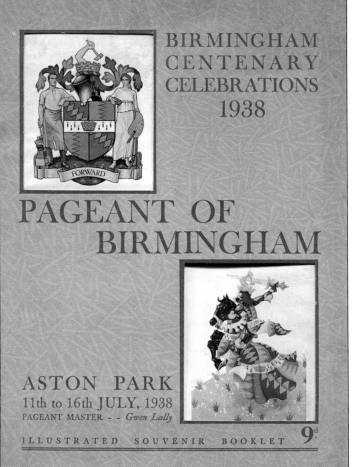

BIRMINGHAM CENTENARY CELEBRATIONS 1938

FORWARD

## PAGEANT OF BIRMINGHAM

ASTON PARK

11th to 16th JULY, 1938

PAGEANT MASTER - - *Gwen Lally*

ILLUSTRATED SOUVENIR BOOKLET  9d

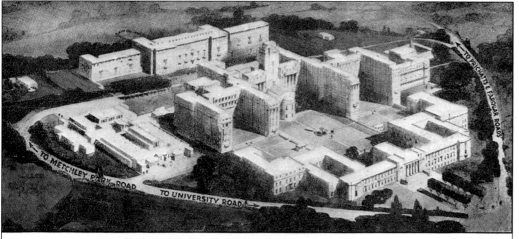

THE BIRMINGHAM HOSPITAL CENTRE, EDGBASTON.
To be opened by H.M. the King on July 14th, 1938.
A scheme for hospital expansion was first mooted some 14 years ago. In 1926 Cadbury Bros. Ltd. gave 150 acres of land, together with an initial sum of £5,000, to assist in the creation of a new hospital away from the congested City centre. Subsequent gifts by the Firm have amounted to a further £60,500. The site adjoins the University, and the scheme will ultimately provide a College of Nursing and new Medical School buildings.

Due to the King's indisposition the Duke and Duchess of Gloucester performed the opening ceremony.

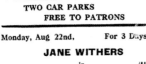

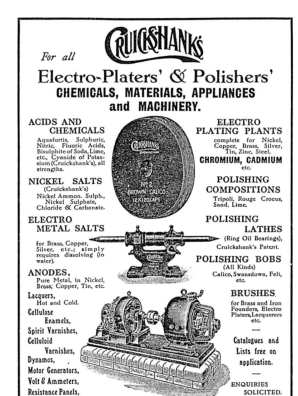

The Prime Minister, Birmingham's Neville Chamberlain, with Italy's Benito Mussolini, at the Munich Conference, 20th September 1938. Afterwards Mr Chamberlain proclaimed that the agreement reached there meant, "Peace in our time". Less than 12 months later we would be at war.

"Football Specials" ready for duty, Garrison Lane, Bordesley, 24th September 1938.

Mill Lane/Digbeth, Deritend, 1938.

## FOR SALE

**Salisbury's,** Radio Engineers have a number of Re-conditioned Radio Bargains from 10/-.—19, Raddlebarn Road, Selly Oak.

**Gent.'s** Modern Compactum: Fitted wardrobe; little used; must be cleared (room wanted). Cost £7/10/-, accept £70/-.—8a, Oak Tree Lane, Selly Oak.

**Auto** Marconiphone Radiogram Model "289." Cost 36gns. as new, will accept 18gns. Also Grandfather chiming clock (two chimes) in perfect condition, cost 20gns., accept £12/10/-.—Enquiries to:-8a, Oak Tree Lane, Selly Oak.

**For Sale** Cheap.—Folding Pram, Child's Cot, Single Bedstead, Toy Pram and Cycle.—Williams, 1653, Pershore Road, Cotteridge.

**Child's Cot;** good condition. Also Folding Pram (Tan Sad).—Apply, 175, Northfield Road, Kings Norton.

**Thorn** Sectional Garden Shed, 10 x 7 x 7, two windows; as new. £3.—71, Clarence Road, Kings Heath.

**Budgerigars;** all colours, from 5/-.—Apply, Sunday before 1 p.m., 85, All Saint's Road.

**1932** Coventry Eagle, 150; 3/4 tax; 150 mp.g.; bargain £4/10/-; evenings.—32, Vicarage Road.

**Belmont** Midget, AC/DC Radio, 4-valve; perfect.—306, Vicarage Road.

**Budgerigars.**—Young hardy outdoor bred birds.—Apply, 295, Brook Lane, Kings Heath.

**Modern,** Double Bed: walnut, well sprung. £1.—Apply, 205, Station Road, Kings Heath.

**Pye,** 4-valve G.B. Wireless: New batteries; absolutely perfect; cost 14gns; accept 39/-.—37, Vicarage Road, Kings Heath. HIGhbury 1749.

At the divisional rally of Deritend Unionist Association a presentation of an illuminated address and a portable wireless is made to Sir John and Lady Smedley Crooke (right) in recognition of their services, Friends' Institute, Moseley Road, 12th October 1938.

The wedding of famous singing duo, Anne Ziegler and Webster Booth, 5th November 1938. Webster was born in Handsworth in 1902.

West Heath Lido, known locally as "The Bath Tub", 1939. Showing the premises of Jarrett, Rainsford and Laughton, (manufacturers of everything, during the war from radios to hand grenades – all very much hush-hush!).

Great Western Arcade, 1939.

Birmingham Corporation Tramway Dept. and Motor Omnibus Garage, Harborne Lane, Selly Oak, 1939.

BIRMINGHAM UNITED HOSPITAL

Visit of Their Majesties

King George VI
and
Queen Elizabeth
to
The Centre Hospital
on
Wednesday, March 1st
1939

## BIRMINGHAM CITY TRANSPORT

*Transport Facilities*

COUNCIL HOUSE,
BIRMINGHAM.

A. C. BAKER
GENERAL MANAGER.

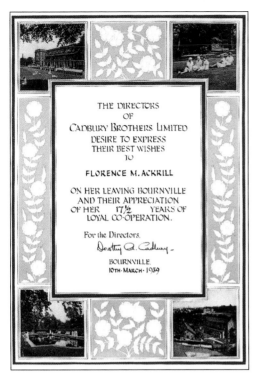

Millpool Hill, Alcester Road South, Kings Heath, 1939.

The Green Man, with Metchley Lane to the left, High Street, Harborne, 1939.
On the corner of Nursery Road can just be seen part of an advertisement for
"If I Were a King" (starring Ronald Colman) at the Royalty.

Yardley Wood Road, Sparkhill, 1939.

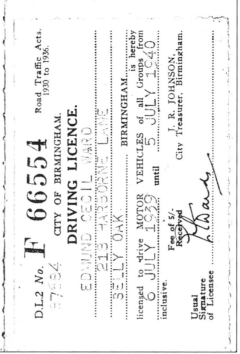

The Duchess of Kent arrives to open Elmdon Airport, 8th July 1939.

# "WE ARE AT WAR

3.9.39

♦

## DRAMATIC SUNDAY BROADCAST

♦

### Premier's It Is a Sad Day For All Of Us

"THIS COUNTRY IS NOW AT WAR WITH GERMANY."

This dramatic announcement was made to the nation by the Prime Minister on Sunday morning in a broadcast at 11.15 a.m.

# BRITAIN AT WAR

## Germany Ignores Final Ultimatum

### Premier's Dramatic Broadcast

# WAR BEGINS
## Poland Invaded; Cities Bombed
### Italy to Keep Out of Conflict

Waiting to be evacuated, Snow Hill Station, September 1939.

In rural areas, during the blackout, some farmers would paint their livestock with white paint in case they strayed into the road, September 1939.

They were issued to all householders with an income of less than £5 per week (£270 today). Higher income householders were charged £7 (£380), 1939.

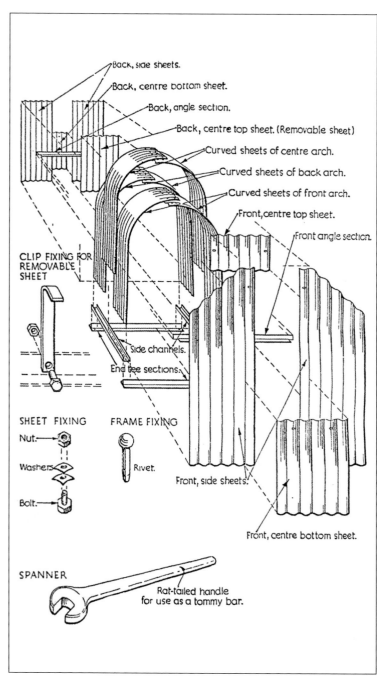

The Grand Priory in the British Realm
of the
Venerable Order of the Hospital of St. John of Jerusalem.
AMBULANCE DEPARTMENT
The St. John Ambulance Association.
(A part of the Red Cross Organization of the British Empire.)

Patron:
HIS MAJESTY THE KING.
(Sovereign Head of the Order.)
President:
H.R.H. THE DUKE OF GLOUCESTER, K.G., etc.
(Grand Prior of the Order.)
Director of Ambulance and Chairman of Committee:
MAJOR-GENERAL SIR PERCIVAL WILKINSON, K.C.M.G., C.B.

This is to Certify that *Ivy Evans*,
has attended a course of Instruction
at the *Birmingham &c* Centre of the Association,
and has qualified to render "First Aid to the Injured."

*[signature]*.
Chief Secretary.

*P. S. Wilkinson.*
Director of Ambulance.

REGISTERED AT ST. JOHN'S GATE, CLERKENWELL, LONDON, E.C.1. *September* 193*7*

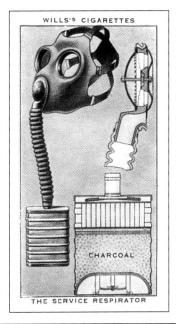

WILLS'S CIGARETTES

CHARCOAL

THE SERVICE RESPIRATOR

HOME OFFICE

## THE PROTECTION OF YOUR HOME AGAINST AIR RAIDS

READ THIS BOOK THROUGH
THEN
KEEP IT CAREFULLY

Dispatch riders line up for inspection, BSA (Birmingham Small Arms) Armory Road, Small Heath, 1939. At the outbreak of war they were the biggest manufacturer of motorcycles in the country.

The King and Queen visit East Works, Austin, Longbridge, 1939.

"Jack and the Beanstalk", with Principal Girl, Dorothy Ward (born in Aston) and the dancers, Alexandra Theatre, 1939.

# How the British Soldier of 1939 Goes to War

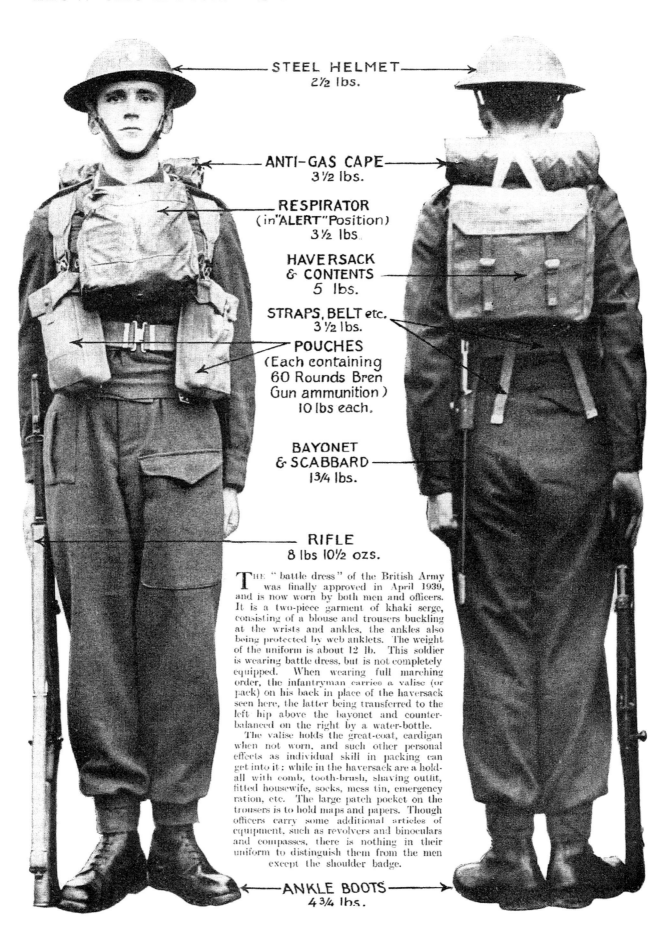

THE "battle dress" of the British Army was finally approved in April 1939, and is now worn by both men and officers. It is a two-piece garment of khaki serge, consisting of a blouse and trousers buckling at the wrists and ankles, the ankles also being protected by web anklets. The weight of the uniform is about 12 lb. This soldier is wearing battle dress, but is not completely equipped. When wearing full marching order, the infantryman carries a valise (or pack) on his back in place of the haversack seen here, the latter being transferred to the left hip above the bayonet and counter-balanced on the right by a water-bottle.

The valise holds the great-coat, cardigan when not worn, and such other personal effects as individual skill in packing can get into it : while in the haversack are a hold-all with comb, tooth-brush, shaving outfit, fitted housewife, socks, mess tin, emergency ration, etc. The large patch pocket on the trousers is to hold maps and papers. Though officers carry some additional articles of equipment, such as revolvers and binoculars and compasses, there is nothing in their uniform to distinguish them from the men except the shoulder badge.

ACKNOWLEDGEMENTS

(for providing photographs, encouragement and numerous other favours)

Keith Ackrill; Norman Bailey; The Birmingham City Council Dept. of Planning and Architecture; The Birmingham Post and Mail Ltd; The Late Gordon Bunce; The Late Arthur Camwell; Roy Dillon; Raymond Horton; Mary Levington; Brian Matthews; Pauline Milner; Dennis Moore; David and Jeanette Parkes; The Late Derek Salberg; Len Scattergood; Keith Shakespeare; Pete Sheldon; Roger Smith; Margaret Spalding; Albert Stanley; Arnie Tyler; The University of Birmingham; June Vaughan; Rosemary Wilkes; Keith Williams; Ken Windsor; Michael Woolley; Eric Wood.


Please forgive any possible omissions. Every effort has been made to include all organisations and individuals involved in the book.

Tony's Red Aces, resident band at Tony's Ballroom, Inge Street, c 1935. They were a regular broadcasting band as well as playing for dancing.